GIVING IT UP FOR LENT

LEADER GUIDE

Bible Study, Drama, Discussion

LINDA BONNEY OLIN

Giving It Up for Lent—Leader Guide: Bible Study, Drama, Discussion

Published by Linda Bonney Olin
New York, USA
www.LindaBonneyOlin.com

ISBN-10: 0991186508
ISBN-13: 978-0-9911865-0-1

CONTENTS

Preface v

Drama: *The Sacrifice Support Group*

    Summary 3

    Act One 5

    Act Two 17

Bible Study and Discussion

    Session One 29

    Session Two 33

    Session Three 35

    Session Four 37

    Session Five 39

Optional Handouts

    Session Two Handout 45

    Session Three Handout 47

    Session Four Handout 49

    Session Five Handout #1 51

    Session Five Handout #2 53

Acknowledgments 55

About the Author 57

PREFACE

I admit it—Pat, the snarky jokester in *The Sacrifice Support Group*, is my alter ego. Which character will *you* identify with most? Melvin, the widowed TV addict? Sandy, the stressed-out snacker? Catherine, the lonely shopaholic? Lee, the image-conscious attorney? Gina, the group's Mother Teresa clone?

Giving It Up for Lent was created to explore the subject of Lenten sacrifice for a weekly supper/study series hosted by an interdenominational cluster of churches in my community. It draws passages from both the Old Testament and the Gospels to show how people offered sacrifices to the Lord in times past—sometimes pleasing him, sometimes not.

The lesson jumps to the present day in *The Sacrifice Support Group*, a two-act dramatic comedy featuring a mixed bag of church characters challenged by their pastor to take a fresh look at the old tradition of giving something up for Lent. Like the fictional characters, study participants will be encouraged to consider offering Lenten sacrifices that glorify the Lord and benefit their families and community—even the world!

The program consists of five weekly sessions. To spread the material over six or seven sessions, split Session One and/or Session Five where indicated.

The play can be performed as Readers Theatre with little or no preparation. The script is set in a larger font for easy reading. Actors with limited mobility can take part, as all characters but one remain seated throughout each act.

This book is designed to be used by the study leader, in conjunction with an individual copy of *Giving It Up for Lent—Workbook: Bible Study, Drama, Discussion* for each study participant. If cost is a concern, handout sheets and scripts may be photocopied from the Leader Guide. Please respect the terms stated on the copyright page.

I hope that *Giving It Up for Lent* will bless you as richly as writing it, acting in *The Sacrifice Support Group*, and leading the study discussion have blessed me. If you enjoy this book, please help spread the word to other readers and leave a review on Amazon.com and Christian book discussion websites. Thanks!

Linda Bonney Olin

Do not forget to do good and to share with others,
for with such sacrifices God is pleased.

Hebrews 13:16

DRAMA

The SACRIFICE Support Group

SUMMARY

Act One: A comically diverse church committee is challenged to put more *giving* into the practice of giving something up for Lent. They form the Sacrifice Support Group to help one another stick to their sacrificial plans. (20 minutes)

Act Two: All members report personal spiritual growth and unexpected joys in addition to the good things they've accomplished for others, inspiring the group to continue the discipline of sacrifice beyond Easter. (20 minutes)

CHARACTERS

PAT ~ Good-hearted woman prone to sarcastic humor. (Can be played as a man.)

MELVIN ~ Blue-collar widowed father who belongs to a service organization. ("Rotarians" can be changed to another organization to suit the audience.)

SANDY ~ Chubby woman who has a tax preparation office in her home.

LEE ~ Female attorney. (Can be played as a male; in that case, change the "girl" in confirmation class to a "young man.")

GINA ~ Shy, devout woman.

CATHERINE ~ Woman wearing a conspicuously ugly outfit or accessories.

PASTOR DALE ~ Clergyperson. (Title can be changed to REVEREND, FATHER, etc.)

SCENE

Church meeting room. A long conference table with seven chairs facing the audience. Small study groups performing the play themselves can simply circle their own chairs.

PROPS

A sheet of paper with printing on it (LEE) and a study Bible (MELVIN). If performing as Readers Theatre, actors can carry their scripts as meeting notes.

ACT ONE

(PAT, MELVIN, and SANDY enter and sit, with MELVIN and SANDY flanking PAT.)

SANDY: I hope this meeting doesn't last too long. This is my busy season, with income taxes and all.

MELVIN: Yeah. I'm gonna miss my favorite TV program if we go over an hour, and I forgot to set the thing to record it.

PAT: We've all got better things to do than hashing over the latest whacky-doodle worship idea. I say we just play along and get it over with, A.S.A.P.

(LEE, GINA, and CATHERINE enter and sit; CATHERINE sits next to LEE.)

LEE: Hi, guys. Let's see … Pat, Melvin, Sandy, Gina, Catherine … looks like we're all here.

MELVIN: Where's Pastor Dale? He's the one who asked us to come.

LEE: Pastor was called to make an urgent hospital visit, so he asked me to sub for him. Basically, he wants the congregation to delve deeper into the tradition of Lenten sacrifice.

PAT: Is he supplying the sackcloth and ashes, or do we have to bring our own?

LEE *(pulling out a paper)*: Here's what Pastor Dale wrote for us. *(Reads.)* "During the upcoming season of Lent, Christians traditionally reflect upon the death of Jesus on the cross, the ultimate model of holiness in his submission to the will of God for the redemption of sinful mankind. This provides an ideal opportunity for each of us to think seriously about how we can emulate our Lord by practicing the spiritual discipline of sacrifice."

PAT: What's to think about? I always give something up for Lent. *(PAT looks around at the others.)* Don't you?

SANDY: Sure. Every year, I give up sweets for Lent.

MELVIN: I give up television.

CATHERINE: I cut back on my shopping trips.

PAT *(to LEE)*: There you go. You can tell Pastor Dale we're all set for Lent. *(PAT rises.)*

LEE *(holding up a hand)*: Not so fast, Pat. *(PAT sits.)* Pastor Dale gave us a list of discussion points. The first one was to share examples of Lenten sacrifices you've made in the past.

PAT: We just covered that. Next!

LEE *(reading from the paper)*: Number two: "Read Hebrews, chapter 13, verses 15 and 16." Catherine, would you read it, please? *(LEE hands CATHERINE the paper.)*

CATHERINE *(reading)*: "Through Jesus, therefore, let us continually offer to God a sacrifice of praise—the fruit of lips that confess his name. And do not forget to do good and to share with others, for with such sacrifices God is pleased." *(She hands the paper back to LEE.)*

PAT: Done!

LEE *(reading)*: "Then discuss the good you've accomplished through your Lenten sacrifices."

SANDY: That's easy. After packing on the pounds over Thanksgiving and Christmas, giving up sweets for Lent helps me get back my girlish figure.

PAT *(loudly aside to MELVIN)*: Never takes her long to lose it again.

SANDY *(a bit defensively)*: Listen, after going without for six weeks, I deserve to pig out on jelly beans and chocolate bunnies. It's Easter tradition.

PAT: Tsk! Tsk! Very bad for your health, Sandy.

SANDY: What do you do, that's so much better?

PAT: I abstain from meat on Fridays. Totally beneficial. I lower my cholesterol, I save a cow, and I keep the local seafood buffets in business. *(piously)* It's a very spiritual discipline, too.

MELVIN *(skeptically)*: How you figure that?

PAT: I always eat at least one helping of grilled fish, just like Jesus cooked for his disciples. I feel closer to our Lord with every bite.

LEE: And you, Catherine? What's the benefit from sacrificing your shopping trips?

CATHERINE: Oh, my budget is always shot after splurging on Christmas gifts and decorations. Lent gives me a chance to save up for the big spring sales.

SANDY *(helpfully)*: The week after Easter is the best time to stock up on discounted candy.

PAT *(loudly aside to SANDY, grinning)*: Catherine doesn't need candy, she needs a new wardrobe. And a fashion consultant to pick it out for her.

LEE: Melvin, what do you do with the time you would have spent watching television?

MELVIN: Well, it opens up a couple hours after supper, before my boys go to bed.

LEE *(approvingly)*: So you make Lent an opportunity to strengthen your family bond.

MELVIN: I guess so. It wears off pretty quick, though.

LEE: Oh?

MELVIN: It takes all my spare time after Easter to watch the TV shows I recorded during Lent. I hardly see the kids for a month.

SANDY: Why don't you watch the shows together?

MELVIN *(sheepishly)*: Umm ... most of the stuff I watch ain't exactly rated G.

PAT *(loudly aside to SANDY)*: Melvin's wife must spin in her grave every time he grabs the remote.

MELVIN: Besides, the kids would rather go their own way most of the time. Be nice to have a tighter relationship with them, but it ain't easy with their mother gone.

SANDY *(sympathetically)*: No, I'm sure it isn't.

LEE: Gina, I didn't hear you say what you give up for Lent.

PAT *(loudly aside to MELVIN)*: I bet Gina gives up dishwashing.

GINA *(shyly)*: I don't exactly give anything up ...

SANDY *(encouragingly)*: Come on, Gina. We're all sharing.

GINA: All right. I guess you could say I gave up fear for Lent.

LEE *(curiously)*: You gave up fear? How do you mean?

GINA: For ages, I felt like God was calling me to do prison ministry, but the idea of going into a jail made me really nervous.

PAT (*loudly aside to SANDY*): She ought to feel right at home there. Half the inmates are her relatives. (*PAT makes a rim-shot gesture.*) Ba-dum-pum, pish!

LEE (*giving PAT a quelling look*): As you were saying, Gina ...

GINA: Finally I decided to put my fear into God's hands and spend every Saturday afternoon helping incarcerated mothers record messages to their kids. Some of the women read a bedtime story into the recorder. Some just say what's in their hearts. Doesn't matter. The idea is to keep their family relationships as strong as possible under the circumstances.

MELVIN: Two thumbs up for that, Gina.

CATHERINE (*impressed*): Yeah. Sounds like a good deed Mother Teresa would do.

LEE: I think that's just the sort of Lent sacrifice Pastor wants to encourage. Giving your time and talents to benefit people in need, instead of the self-serving sacrifices Christians usually make. To be honest, that's the main reason I've never done the sacrifice bit for Lent. It always seemed so hypocritical.

PAT: Self-serving sacrifices? That's an oxymoron. Oh, sorry, Gina, I shouldn't cut you out of the conversation by using five-dollar words. I meant, it's a contradiction.

SANDY: We all know what you meant, Pat. A sacrifice can't be selfish.

CATHERINE (*thoughtfully*): I'm not so sure. Lee might actually have a good angle there.

PAT: Lee's a lawyer. They always have a good angle.

CATHERINE: No, really. You heard our sacrifices. Some of the things we said we gave up for Lent, we really just postponed until after Easter.

PAT: Like Melvin recording his cable shows to watch later?

CATHERINE: Well, yeah. And my shopping sprees.

SANDY: Oh ... I guess the same goes for my candy.

CATHERINE: Afraid so, Sandy.

SANDY: And the benefit of cutting out sweets was to look slimmer, which is all about myself, basically. Is that what you're getting at?

MELVIN *(to LEE)*: I thought I was doing a good thing, giving up TV for Lent. You saying I made a bad sacrifice?

LEE: Look, I'm not throwing stones here. I've never sacrificed for Lent, so you're all miles ahead of me.

SANDY: Come on, guys. We won't get anywhere by turning on Lee.

CATHERINE: Or beating ourselves up for making mistakes in the past. But where do we go from here?

PAT: Call me radical, but how about we go to the next item on that list, so we can blast out of here before Melvin misses another hour of quality television programming.

LEE: All right. *(LEE reads.)* Number three: "How might you benefit others this year with the time, treasure, or other resources you free up by making your Lenten sacrifice?"

SANDY: Others? You mean like sharing my Easter candy with the poor?

LEE: That would be one way.

SANDY *(dismayed)*: But looking forward to my chocolate binge is the only thing that keeps me going during Lent. You don't know how hard it is for me to lay off the sweets when I'm stressed out, and "stress" is my middle name during tax season.

GINA *(quietly)*: I've found the Lord always gives me the strength to endure any hardship for his sake, especially when I'm doing good for people who are worse off than I am.

PAT *(snidely)*: Yeah, Sandy. Listen to Mother Teresa over there.

SANDY *(fed up, but not harshly)*: You know, Pat, I wish you'd give up sarcasm for Lent.

PAT: You don't get to pick another person's sacrifice, Sandy. Too bad, 'cause if it was up to me ...

SANDY: I'm serious. If you gave up making snide remarks for six weeks, the whole town would benefit.

MELVIN: If Pat quit making fun of people, the whole town wouldn't recognize her.

PAT: Lighten up. I'm only kidding. Jesus poked fun at people, too, you know.

CATHERINE: Only when they deserved it, to teach them a lesson. Nobody here deserves your wisecracks, especially Gina.

MELVIN: Yeah, Gina don't need a lesson. She's already making a good sacrifice.

PAT *(sarcastically)*: Well, all hail to Saint Gina, for teaching the rest of us the true meaning of Lent!

SANDY: There you go again! I know you're trying to be comical, but those little jabs hurt.

PAT *(defensively)*: And I'm supposed to enjoy your criticizing me?

LEE: Take it easy, Pat. We're just trying to learn from one another.

PAT: Well, you can do it without me if you're going to get touchy every time I open my mouth. *(PAT flounces out of the meeting room, griping toward the audience as she leaves.)* Talk about thin skin ...

(SANDY rises as if to follow PAT.)

CATHERINE: Let her go, Sandy.

(SANDY sits. PAT stops where she can be seen by the audience, and eavesdrops on the meeting with her hand cupped around her ear.)

MELVIN: That was fairly humorous.

CATHERINE: Moving right along ... What else is on Pastor's paper?

LEE: Just a few more points for reflection. *(LEE reads.)* "True sacrifices are voluntary, not forced ... Give up something of great value for a greater good ... Choose a sacrifice that has personal significance ..."

GINA: Yes. Pat was right when she said you can't pick other people's sacrifices.

(PAT nods smugly.)

MELVIN: Makes sense. I'm more likely to do something tough, if I buy into it.

SANDY: I agree. The tricky part is that "greater good."

CATHERINE: Yeah. I always thought the purpose of denying yourself during Lent was to grow holier by suffering.

SANDY: And to remind yourself to be grateful for God's gift of chocolate, right? *(The others look at SANDY. She shrugs.)* Or television, or shopping, or whatever.

LEE: I don't think those are bad intentions, as far as they go. Pastor Dale just wants us to step up to a higher level.

GINA: I do like the idea of using our sacrifices to make the world a better place.

MELVIN, SANDY, CATHERINE: Me, too.

LEE: After all, the goal is to follow the example of Jesus, and that's what Jesus did. I mean, he didn't die on the cross just for the sake of dying. He did it out of love, and his death accomplished something big for the world.

(PAT reacts, looking thoughtful.)

CATHERINE: It doesn't get much bigger than eternal life.

SANDY: That's the truth.

(PAT nods.)

LEE: Okay. On that note, can we agree to give prayerful consideration to making a truly significant Lenten sacrifice this year? Think about what you have of value and how you could benefit others if you give it up. *(LEE glares around at the group.)* Really give it up.

MELVIN: We hear you. Hmm ... Is it okay to give up the same thing we sort of gave up before?

LEE: That's your personal decision, remember?

MELVIN *(thoughtfully)*: Unplugging the boob tube to make time for my kids was on the right track. If I do that again, plus give up recording my shows for later ...

GINA: Have you ever considered spending some of that extra time studying scriptures?

MELVIN: I ain't opened our family Bible in ages. Can't stand all them begats, and thees, and thous. To say nothing of the mile-long names in there.

GINA: They make different Bibles now that use modern language, easy for regular people to read. My ladies at the jail use a kids' Bible to tape Bible stories for their children.

SANDY: There's something you could do with your kids, Melvin.

MELVIN (*doubtfully*): They're teenage boys. Bible study ain't their idea of a good time.

GINA: You might be surprised.

MELVIN: I'll think about it, but I ain't making no promises.

CATHERINE: Sandy, you and I could give the money we save on sweets and shopping to charity, instead of pampering ourselves with after-Easter binges.

SANDY (*with growing enthusiasm*): Yeah ... Or, if I can't look forward to a chocolate binge for myself, maybe planning an Easter candy blowout for underprivileged kids would keep me motivated during Lent. (*SANDY turns to GINA.*) Gina, are you going to do your jail thing this Lent?

GINA: Yes.

SANDY: Terrific! If I fill and decorate a few Easter baskets, could you arrange delivery to the prison ladies' children?

GINA: I'd love to!

CATHERINE: Good idea. That adds a lot more personal significance than just mailing a check. Now, what could I do? (*Thinks, then snaps her fingers as an idea strikes her.*) Hey, I wouldn't mind shopping for people who can't do it themselves. (*She frowns.*) Wait. Would that be a selfish sacrifice since I enjoy shopping?

GINA: No, I think the Lord likes us to get pleasure from helping others.

SANDY (*enthusiastically*): This is great, bouncing ideas off each other.

MELVIN: Especially, not having the class clown here making fun of them.

(*PAT looks shamefaced.*)

LEE: Pastor Dale will be thrilled that you're all willing to stretch your thinking.

GINA: What about you, Lee?

LEE: Good question. I have to start from scratch, since I wasn't doing anything for Lent before.

CATHERINE: We've covered lots of possibilities you could choose from. Doing good for others by giving up time, money, favorite foods and activities …

SANDY: Giving up fear. That was real creative, Gina.

LEE: Yes, it was. People could certainly free themselves for a lot of worthwhile things if they gave up the negative attitudes that hold them back.

CATHERINE: Like prejudice.

SANDY: Or worrying. If I gave up fretting about my workload, I'd free up a lot of energy.

GINA: How about giving up pride? You know. Humbling ourselves to be the first to say, "I'm sorry."

(*At that, PAT straightens up, then slumps and frowns.*)

CATHERINE: Plain old indifference to the next guy's problems is a big negative.

MELVIN: Yeah. Channel-surfing the other night, I caught a program telling how thousands of babies die in what they call "convenience abortions." (*He shakes his head in disbelief.*) People would rather look the other way than do something about it.

LEE: I've always thought it was a terrible injustice. But I don't see myself marching around with a sign in front of abortion clinics. Can you imagine, if my clients were to see me?

GINA: Isn't it more important to imagine where God wants to see you?

(*PAT straightens up, looking resolute.*)

LEE: Ouch! Guess I'm guilty of hypocrisy myself. (*LEE pauses to consider.*) Hmm …

(*PAT walks toward the meeting room as the conversation continues.*)

SANDY: A person with your legal skills would be a wonderful advocate for those babies.

LEE: That's true ... Okay, here goes, before I chicken out. As my Lent sacrifice, I hereby commit myself to helping defend the unborn, wherever God wants me to do it.

GINA: Good for you, Lee!

CATHERINE: You're setting a brave example, diving headfirst into unfamiliar water like that.

PAT *(walking into the room)*: Splash! Glub, glub, glub ... *(The others stare at PAT.)* That's the sound of me belly-flopping into the deep end along with Lee.

MELVIN *(rolling his eyes)*: All right, what's the punch line?

PAT: No joke. Sulking out there by myself gave me time to think. *(PAT smiles ruefully.)* Maybe gave the Holy Spirit a chance to get a word in edgewise, too.

LEE *(warily)*: Oh? What did he have to say?

PAT: That you guys were right. My so-called comedy is unfair and unkind. And I acted like a two-year-old, stomping out of the room like that. I'm truly sorry.

(The others look at one another with raised eyebrows.)

SANDY: Are you promising to stop making jokes at other people's expense?

PAT: Yup. That's going to be my new Lenten sacrifice. *(flippantly)* Even though you picked it for me. *(PAT pauses and looks crestfallen.)* Oops. Quitting sarcasm cold turkey could be tougher than I thought. I don't know if I can do it on my own. Would you be willing to pray for me? And call me to account when I slip up?

(The others look at one another for several seconds. Then SANDY nods her head decisively.)

SANDY: Absolutely! Will you do the same for me?

CATHERINE: Count me in.

MELVIN: Me too. We're all going to need help to keep going with this sacrifice discipline.

LEE: What do you think about getting together once a week to share our experiences as we go along?

SANDY: Like a sacrifice support group?

CATHERINE: Yeah!

GINA: The six of us plus the Holy Spirit, praying for strength and guidance. How can we miss?

PAT: You're very gracious to include me and my big mouth.

SANDY: You have a big heart, too, Pat. That's what counts.

LEE: And guess what? You just illustrated the final item on Pastor's list. A closing prayer from Psalm 51 for us to meditate on until we meet again. Here, Pat. You read it. *(LEE hands PAT the paper.)*

PAT: "The sacrifice God wants is a broken spirit. God, you will not reject a heart that is broken and sorry for sin." Amen to that!

ALL: Amen!

End of Act One

ACT TWO

(ALL enter and sit. MELVIN carries a Bible bookmarked to Genesis 18:19.)

LEE *(looking around)*: Pat, Melvin, Sandy, Gina, Catherine ... Looks like the gang's all here.

PASTOR: Thanks for letting me sit in on your meeting. I'm very interested to hear your experiences after five weeks of practicing the spiritual discipline of sacrifice.

PAT: I have to admit, Pastor Dale, when you first asked us to think more deeply about sacrificing for Lent, I couldn't imagine what there was to think about. Boy, have I learned a lot!

CATHERINE: We were pretty misguided about the things we'd been giving up for Lent.

LEE: Not me.

PASTOR: Oh?

LEE *(shrugging sheepishly)*: Only because I'd never done any kind of Lenten discipline.

SANDY: To be honest, what most of us were doing hardly qualified as "discipline" at all. I gave up sweets during Lent, but I made up for lost time as soon as Easter rolled around.

CATHERINE: Same for me and my shopping.

MELVIN: And my television shows.

PAT: My abstaining from meat on Fridays actually translated to trading hamburgers for seafood once a week. Not what you'd call hard-core fasting.

PASTOR: I understand you all discussed the material I gave you, and made a commitment to choose Lenten sacrifices with a purpose this year.

LEE: Yes, giving up something significant to benefit others, like you suggested, Pastor.

PAT: But it didn't take long to realize we needed each other's help to stick with our plans, so we agreed to meet here every week for mutual support.

17

SANDY: The Sacrifice Support Group, we call it.

PASTOR: That was a great idea. So, let's hear how your sacrifices are going. Gina, I know you took a recorder to the county jail on a weekly basis during Lent last year, to help incarcerated mothers create messages to their kids. You did that again this year, right?

GINA: Actually, I had never stopped doing it. The personal connections I made were too precious to walk away from after Easter. But this year I'm adding a new twist, thanks to Sandy.

PASTOR (*turning to SANDY*): Oh?

SANDY: At first, all I intended to do for my new and improved sacrifice was to pick a charity and donate the money I saved from giving up candy for Lent. But that seemed awfully impersonal. So I asked Gina about donating Easter goodies for her prison ladies and their children.

GINA: You should see the pile of Easter baskets Sandy has ready for me to deliver. They take up two rooms in her house.

SANDY: They're spilling over into my home tax office now, too. I was having such a ball decorating and stuffing the baskets and saying a prayer for the person who'd receive each one, I decided to do up a bunch for the Domestic Violence Shelter, too.

PAT: That's fantastic, Sandy.

SANDY: It's weird. I never thought I could fast from sweets for five whole weeks without bribing myself with an I.O.U. for chocolate bunnies and jellybeans. This year, I'm too excited about giving goodies away to feel deprived. Or stressed out by my tax work, either.

MELVIN: If you don't mind my saying, I can tell by looking, you've dropped some weight in the process.

SANDY (*nonchalant, but pleased*): You're probably right.

CATHERINE: "Probably"? Haven't you been jumping on the scale to track every ounce?

SANDY: Nope. The idea was to sacrifice for the kids, not for my looks.

PAT: It'll be good for your health that you're planning to keep those pounds off, this time around.

SANDY: Yup. No more Easter candy pig-outs for me.

LEE: Catherine, you modified your original plan, too. Tell Pastor Dale about that.

CATHERINE: Well, in the past, all the cash I saved by giving up recreational shopping during Lent just got shopped away after Easter. So I had the same idea as Sandy, to donate my savings to charity this year. But instead, I've used the money to gas up my car for more shopping runs.

PASTOR: You lost me. Where's the sacrifice?

CATHERINE: Admittedly, it's not much of a sacrifice, considering that shopping is my favorite hobby, but ... instead of mall-hopping for myself, I go shopping for a dozen homebound elderly women.

PASTOR: Excellent!

CATHERINE: Actually, I'm enjoying this project so much, I'm making it permanent, like Gina.

PASTOR: Even better.

CATHERINE: Not having a family, my time is flexible. Good thing, too. My ladies love to chat when I deliver their bags.

GINA (*nodding*): That's those precious connections I was talking about. Your caring means so much to folks who can't get out and around.

MELVIN: Speaking of getting out and around, I been a lot more active since I gave up watching and recording TV shows.

GINA: Doing things with your children?

MELVIN: Yup. We been going out for music and sports, museums, all kinds of fun stuff. The kids ain't smiled this much since their mom passed away.

PAT: She's smiling ear to ear in heaven, watching you being such a dedicated dad, Melvin.

MELVIN: Yeah, maybe she is. Especially on our Bible study nights.

LEE, **CATHERINE**, **PAT**, **SANDY** (*astonished*): What?

MELVIN: Remember, that was Gina's bright idea, that me and the kids ought to read the Bible together. So I had her get us one of them study Bibles for kids like she told us about. *(MELVIN holds up his Bible.)* No more thees, and thous, and begats.

SANDY: How'd your boys like it?

MELVIN: They think it's cool, how it's got notes at the bottom to explain what you're reading, and extra pages in the back—you know, maps and pictures and stuff. Makes it real interesting. Even those weird names are kind of fun to look up.

GINA *(pleased)*: I knew you'd be hooked if you gave it a try.

MELVIN: We made it most of the way through Genesis already. Man, the families in there make us look good.

PASTOR: Reading those stories with your kids gives you a handy opening to talk about morality issues.

MELVIN: Yeah, and me and my sons needed that. It was like God was talking about me when he said ... Hold on, I marked it ... *(He opens his Bible to the bookmark.)* Here we go. Genesis, chapter 18, verse 19. "I have chosen him, so that he will direct his children and his household after him to keep the way of the Lord by doing what is right and just." And another one I ran across. Joshua, chapter 24, verse 15. "But as for me and my household, we will serve the Lord." I liked that one so much I memorized it.

CATHERINE: Wow, Melvin. I am impressed.

LEE, SANDY, PASTOR, PAT: Yeah!

MELVIN: I got to say, trading TV time for family time may have started out being a sacrifice for Lent, but I made up my mind, this is the way life is gonna be in our house, for good.

SANDY: I've been praying every day for you and the kids, Melvin. It's a real joy to hear you've turned a corner.

MELVIN: Thanks, Sandy. I believe we have. *(MELVIN looks around at the group, grinning.)* Oh, hey. I got to tell you guys about something me and my boys got a big kick out of the other night. Right, Pat?

PAT *(grinning)*: Oh, yeah! I had Melvin laughing so hard at one point, we put the emergency squad on standby.

SANDY *(dismayed)*: Oh, no! After all the prayers I've said, you didn't go back to making fun of people, did you?

PAT: Only myself, and the world at large. No personal slams, don't worry.

PASTOR: What's this?

PAT: You know me, Pastor. Everything strikes me funny, and I got into the habit of giving a running commentary to get a laugh. In fact, I was on quite a roll at our first meeting here.

MELVIN, SANDY, CATHERINE: I'll say!

PAT: Until these friends, and the Holy Spirit, pointed out that my witticisms were really hurtful. So, I gave up wisecracking for Lent.

PASTOR: That's a tough resolution to keep.

PAT: It certainly didn't come easy, seeing silly things all around me and having to keep my lip zipped. *(PAT frowns.)* And it just didn't feel right. I thought, I know Jesus has a sense of humor, so joking can't be all bad, can it? And what Catherine and Gina said at our first meeting, that God likes to see us enjoy what we do for other people? Suddenly it all came together, and I took the plunge.

MELVIN: Pat volunteered to do a stand-up comedy act at a variety show my service club held last week, to benefit disaster victims. She was a riot.

SANDY *(wide-eyed)*: You got up in front of an actual live audience and told jokes?

GINA: Yow! I'd never have the guts to do that.

PAT *(wryly)*: I don't think telling jokes to a roomful of charity donors takes more guts than your jail ministry, Gina.

GINA: It would for me!

MELVIN: And I can testify, Pat kept her Lent promise. She told funny stories, without one single mean jab.

PAT: I asked the Holy Spirit to help me put together ten minutes of funny material that was un-mean and squeaky clean. Needless to say, he came through for me.

PASTOR: Sounds like you found the experience satisfying, and you certainly benefited people in need by performing at a fundraiser.

MELVIN: I wish other comedians could see Pat getting belly laughs with her G-rated routine. They might clean up their acts. (*He shakes his head in disgust.*) Man, you should hear the comics on cable.

CATHERINE: Rather not, thanks. Half their stuff gets bleeped, and the other half ought to.

LEE: Melvin's right, Pat. There's potential here for a much broader positive impact.

GINA (*to PAT*): Do you think you'd be interested in doing more comedy gigs?

PAT (*smiling*): Considering it took six Rotarians to wrestle the microphone away when my ten minutes were up, I'd say there's a decent possibility.

SANDY: Cool! Save the front row for the Sacrifice Support Group.

PAT: With pleasure.

PASTOR: Lee, tell me about your Lent experience.

LEE: I picked up on something Melvin said at our first meeting, about unborn babies dying by the thousands. To make a long story short, I decided to give up my indifference for Lent.

PASTOR: That's a great concept, but how did you put it into action?

LEE: Well, here's where the story gets longer. When I made my commitment, I said I'd follow God's leading to defend the unborn. And I meant that. But I was afraid God would expect me to march in front of abortion clinics carrying protest signs, and I really hate making a public spectacle of myself. So I approached him with a counterproposal.

(*PAT claps her hands over her own mouth and looks at the ceiling.*)

CATHERINE (*smiling at PAT*): Since Pat can't say it, I will: Leave it to a lawyer to negotiate with God!

LEE: That's just it, I'm a lawyer. I offered God my legal skills, to advocate for legislation against convenience abortions, and for health care that would give all babies a better chance to survive.

PASTOR: That seems like a perfectly acceptable offering.

LEE *(wryly)*: That's probably what Cain said. Just before God lowered the boom on him.

MELVIN *(pointing to his Bible)*: Me and the boys read about Cain in here. His brother offered God the very best from his animals and God was happy. Then Cain offered some of his harvest but God got mad because Cain held back his best stuff. Right?

GINA: That pretty much says it.

PASTOR: And you feel Cain's story applies to you, Lee?

LEE: Regrettably, yes. By offering God only the services I could provide from a cushy seat in my office, I was holding back my best stuff, like Cain did. God wanted me to sacrifice my white-collar comfort zone, and follow his marching orders.

PASTOR: Marching in abortion protests?

LEE: Just the opposite. The Holy Spirit prodded me to go private, not public.

PASTOR: How do you mean?

LEE: Well, while I was doing the research to prepare for legislative lobbying, it started to sink in that those statistics are real people, not just numbers. Every unborn baby who dies through abortion or malnutrition or lack of medical care is a real child, with a real mother and a real father. And I thought about the kids in our own community, in this very church, who become those statistics. I asked God, "Why are unmarried Christian teens getting pregnant in the first place? Are they so hungry for love? So broken? And what can one person do about such a huge problem?" And God said, "Yes, you are only one person, but so is every baby. So is every unloved, broken teenager. Help them, one by one. That's the best you can offer me." *(LEE pauses several seconds to compose her emotions before continuing.)* I'd barely recovered from that revelation when my phone rang.

GINA *(to PASTOR)*: Remember, we had one girl who wanted to be in our spring confirmation class, but no one was willing to mentor her? Something told me to call Lee. I was all ready to make my pitch and get turned down. Again. But Lee agreed right away to be her mentor.

CATHERINE *(to LEE)*: Better you than me.

MELVIN: Yeah. I've seen her at school. Heard her, I should say. That kid has a mouth on her that would give Pat a run for her money. *(MELVIN looks apologetically at PAT.)* The old Pat, that is.

PAT: That's okay, I know what you mean, Melvin. The cops are all the time getting called out to her foster home. A sad situation, really.

GINA: Yet she comes to church almost every Sunday.

SANDY: Yes. I've been praying for her, sitting all by herself in a back pew.

GINA: She put her own name on the signup sheet for confirmation. That was quite a big step.

PASTOR *(to LEE)*: It's a big step for you, too, Lee. You understand this is a long-term relationship you're taking on, not just a few weeks' commitment for Lent.

LEE: One by one, the Lord said. And she's the one. However long it takes.

PASTOR: I think this is going to be an exhilarating challenge for both of you.

SANDY *(looking around with dawning realization)*: Say … Does that make me the only one of the group who's only sacrificing until Easter?

(The group looks around at one another.)

CATHERINE: Looks that way.

PASTOR: And that's all right, Sandy. There was no obligation as to what kind of sacrifice to make or how long it should last.

SANDY: But hearing about all your plans really whets my appetite.

PAT *(grinning)*: Must you tempt me with straight lines like that, when I've sworn off making snappy comebacks?

SANDY *(smiling)*: I was referring to my appetite for the joy, and exhilaration, and precious connections you're all going to get from God working in your lives, while I wait until next year.

PASTOR: You don't have to.

SANDY *(scoffing)*: Easter baskets would look kind of silly on the Fourth of July.

PASTOR: I meant, you could continue the discipline of sacrifice without necessarily continuing the same sacrifice you made during Lent.

GINA: Sandy, you're always welcome in the prison ministry, with or without candy baskets.

CATHERINE: Or you can go shopping with me.

LEE: I don't suppose you'd care to hit the comedy stage with Pat.

SANDY: Not a chance!

PAT: Well, you certainly don't need to give up sarcasm, like I did. You're one of the most encouraging people I know.

LEE, PASTOR, MELVIN, GINA, CATHERINE: Yeah.

GINA: I don't know how we'd all get along without your prayers.

MELVIN: That's it!

LEE: What?

MELVIN *(to SANDY)*: You said prayers over your Easter baskets, right?

SANDY: Yeah, for the people who are going to get them.

MELVIN: And you been praying nonstop for every member of the Sacrifice Support Group, right? And for that girl Lee's working with?

SANDY: Well, sure. Better praying than snacking.

MELVIN: So you're already a partner in all our sacrifices. You don't have to do the same stuff everybody else does. Just keep them prayers coming.

PAT, CATHERINE, GINA, LEE: Yeah!

(SANDY looks questioningly at PASTOR, as if seeking his approval.)

PASTOR: Certainly—prayer is a discipline that pleases the Lord.

SANDY: I'll be glad to do that. And you'll all share your ups and downs with me?

PAT, **MELVIN**, **CATHERINE**, **GINA**, **LEE**: Yes!

CATHERINE: Since our sacrifices are continuing beyond Easter, how about keeping the Sacrifice Support Group going, too? Maybe meet once a month until next Lent?

PAT, **MELVIN**, **SANDY**, **GINA**, **LEE**: Yeah!

PASTOR: Then join hands and let me send you on your way with a few words of blessing borrowed from Paul's first letter to the Thessalonians. *(Pause as ALL join hands.)* "God did not appoint us to suffer wrath but to receive salvation through our Lord Jesus Christ. He died for us so that we may live together with him. Therefore encourage one another and build each other up, just as in fact you are doing. Do not put out the Spirit's fire. May God himself, the God of peace, sanctify you through and through. The grace of our Lord Jesus Christ be with you."

ALL: Amen.

End of Act Two

BIBLE STUDY

AND

DISCUSSION

SESSION ONE

Open and close each session with prayer.

LEADER:

In this study, we're going to take a new look at a very old tradition, that of offering sacrifices to the Lord God. The Bible's first account of this form of worship is found in the Book of Genesis.

Read Genesis 4:1–7. (Scriptures may be read by Leader or by participants.)

Abel offered the choicest cuts from the firstborn of his flocks, showing that he gave the Lord first place in his life. The Lord was pleased with Abel's sacrifice. The Bible tells us that Cain offered *some* of the produce he'd harvested from the soil. Not the best. Not the first. The Lord rejected Cain's offering. Clearly, mankind's first lesson in sacrifices was to honor the Lord God with the very best you had to give.

Read Genesis 22:1–18.

The Lord gave Abraham detailed instructions for this sacrifice. Abraham obeyed without question. What faithful submission to the will of God! At the very moment Abraham raised his knife, God intervened and spared Isaac's life. It was enough that Abraham proved to be willing to give up everything he had for his sovereign Lord, even his beloved son.

As Abraham's descendants grew into the great nation the Lord had promised, the Lord taught them more about how, when, and why to offer sacrifices to him. He established rules for ritual offerings of valuable items such as animals, grain, wine, and oil. Only the most perfect specimens, carefully examined and certified to be without blemish, were set aside for sacrificial purposes. Specific offerings were prescribed to glorify God, to petition God for his protection and provision, to thank God for blessings granted, to purify the people, and to atone for their sins.

But rules were not enough. Ritual sacrifices became token displays of righteousness while the people lived unrighteous lives, enriching themselves at the expense of the powerless and worshipping the idols of neighboring cultures. Even their leaders were guilty of offering hypocritical sacrifices.

Read 1 Samuel 15:1–26.

The arrogant Saul learned the hard way that burning animal offerings on an altar was no substitute for obeying the Lord. The Lord rejected Saul as King of Israel. Other prophets repeatedly warned the people that their sinful behavior made their offerings unacceptable to the Lord.

Read Isaiah 1:11–17 and Micah 6:6–8.

Like the prophets before him, Jesus Christ called for the sacrifice of obedient living. He modeled a holy lifestyle of self-denial in fasting and prayer. He devoted himself to humbly serving both God and people. He called his disciples' attention to an offering that looked tiny to the world but was large in God's eyes because it represented great cost to the humble giver.

Read Mark 12:41–44.

The perfect culmination of the sacrificial tradition was the death of Jesus himself, the unblemished Lamb of God, on the cross. Jesus gave his life in atonement for the sins of the world, glorifying God through his obedience and gaining everlasting life for all who believe.

Two thousand years later, what is the Lord trying to teach us through these Bible lessons? Does sacrifice still please God? Is the concept of self-denial relevant in this self-indulgent age?

In modern times, many Christians have sought to emulate the spirit of sacrifice shown by Jesus Christ by offering personal sacrifices to God during Lent—not slaughtering animals or burning crops on an altar, but voluntarily giving up some cherished possession or pleasurable activity. But, for those in our group who've been observing this tradition, has "giving it up for Lent" become a stale routine? Even worse, are we, like the Hebrews, guilty of offering token sacrifices to God while going about our self-serving business as usual?

This study will explore those questions.

To spread the study program over more shorter sessions, divide Session One into two sessions, ending the first half here.

LEADER:

Can we give the age-old discipline of Lenten sacrifice fresh meaning by bringing the Lord personal offerings that have significant value and purpose? Here's a look at a fictional church group faced with that challenge.

DRAMA:

Perform The Sacrifice Support Group, Act One.

LEADER:

We'll look in on the Sacrifice Support Group in a later session to see how they fared with their new and improved Lenten intentions.

Over the coming days, let's prayerfully consider how we might enrich our Lenten worship with an approach to sacrifice that is centered on God and neighbor. Like the character of Pat in our drama, we may need to make some quiet time to allow the Holy Spirit to get a word in edgewise. And like the fictional Sacrifice Support Group, we'll meet again to discuss our progress and encourage one another.

SESSION TWO

Answers to the refresher questions about the drama are provided here in italics for the Leader's reference while guiding the discussion.

LEADER:

1. In the first act of *The Sacrifice Support Group*, you met six fictional Christians challenged by their pastor to re-think their ideas about Lenten sacrifice. What did we learn about these characters and their previous Lenten practices?

   o *Sandy, who is always stressed during Lent because it coincides with her hectic income tax season, gave up sweets for Lent. But she treated herself to a big basket of candy as soon as Lent was over.*

   o *Catherine cut back on her shopping trips during Lent to save money for future spending sprees.*

   o *Melvin, the widowed father of several teenage sons, gave up watching television during Lent. However, he recorded his programs to watch later, with the result that he hardly saw his boys for weeks after Easter.*

   o *Pat, the jokester of the group, was quite smug about abstaining from meat on Fridays during Lent. Pat went to the seafood buffet instead.*

   o *Gina, a shy woman, gave up her fear and ministered to incarcerated women and their families.*

   o *Lee, the attorney, has never offered a Lenten sacrifice, believing Christians are hypocritical in the way they give things up for Lent.*

2. Do you see any truth in Lee's opinion that Christians make "self-serving sacrifices"?

3. What new or improved sacrifices did each person commit to make?

- o *Sandy plans to give up sweets again. But she'll treat disadvantaged kids, not herself, to candy baskets this Easter.*

- o *Catherine, the shopaholic, will still cut back on recreational shopping, but she'll give the money she saves to charity. She might also volunteer to do shopping for other people.*

- o *Melvin will give up watching and recording TV during Lent to spend more time with his sons. He did not agree to read the Bible with them as Gina suggested.*

- o *Pat promised to give up making hurtful wisecracks.*

- o *Gina will repeat her jail ministry.*

- o *Lee will give up indifference, vowing to advocate for unborn babies.*

4. Whose sacrifice do you think will be the hardest for him/her to accomplish? The easiest? Why?

5. Which of these characters' planned sacrifices would pose the most difficulty for you to do? Why? Which of their sacrifices would pose the least difficulty for you to do? Why?

6. Consider the things that the group is going to give up. How had those things come between them and God? Between them and other people?

7. The group observed that giving up fear, prejudice, anxiety, indifference, and pride could free individuals to do good things. Can you think of other negative attitudes that hold Christians back from serving God and their neighbors?

8. Can you suggest good sacrifice choices that were not mentioned in the play?

9. The fictional Sacrifice Support Group members promised to call one another to account when they slipped up. How would you feel about giving and receiving that kind of input?

SESSION THREE

LEADER:

Read Matthew 6:1–6, 16–18.

Jesus cautioned his disciples not to publicly display their charitable giving, praying, and fasting. Certainly, boasting about virtuous acts won't earn any credit in heaven. However, within this group, we'll be invited to share our personal experiences—not to show off our sackcloth and ashes, but to encourage and learn from one another. In that spirit, if you're comfortable doing so, please share your own experiences freely in response to our discussion questions.

If the group is large, Leader may choose to have participants discuss the following questions in breakout groups.

LEADER:

1. What are some examples of Lenten sacrifices you have made in the past?

2. Have you felt inspired to make a new or improved Lenten sacrifice commitment this year?

3. What have you chosen to sacrifice? What will you do with the time, treasure, or other resources your sacrifice frees up? Or does your sacrifice involve doing more rather than giving something up?

4. How do you expect your sacrifice to benefit others?

5. Other questions or thoughts to share?

6. Before our next session, find a passage in the New Testament which provides guidance regarding sacrifice. Bring it in to share with the group.

Leader also should prepare a passage or two. Jot them in the space below.

SESSION FOUR

Invite participants to read and discuss the sacrifice-related New Testament passages they've brought in. Leader also can read passages he/she has prepared.

If the group is large, Leader may choose to have participants discuss the following questions in breakout groups.

LEADER:

1. What form has your Lenten sacrifice taken?

2. Was the cherished thing you gave up coming between you and God? Will giving it up strengthen you and/or your family, church, or community?

3. How does your sacrifice glorify God? Can sacrifices made in secret give glory to God?

4. Have any problems hindered your sacrificial plans? Were they overcome?

Give participants an opportunity to offer helpful suggestions and encouragement to one another.

5. Has confiding your sacrifice plan to this group or to a trusted friend helped you carry it out?

6. Have you seen God working in your life or the lives of others as a result of your sacrificial acts?

7. What are you learning about yourself during this process? About other people? About God?

8. According to the gospel of John, the last words of Jesus on the cross were a loud cry of victory: "It is finished!" Have you ever felt a sense of spiritual victory upon completing a difficult task in obedience to God's direction?

9. Other questions or thoughts to share?

SESSION FIVE

LEADER:

Several weeks ago, we challenged ourselves to re-think the traditional discipline of Lenten sacrifice and to consider offering significant sacrifices with a godly purpose. We looked at a fictional church group who took up the same challenge. Now we're going to check on their progress.

DRAMA:

Perform The Sacrifice Support Group, Act Two.

Answers to the recap questions are provided here in italics for the Leader's reference while guiding the discussion.

LEADER:

1. How well did *The Sacrifice Support Group* characters succeed in carrying out their Lenten sacrifice commitments?

   o *Everyone succeeded.*

   o *Several were inspired to accomplish even more than they had planned.*

2. How did their Lenten activities benefit others?

   o *Incarcerated women and their children stayed in touch thanks to Gina's ministry and will receive Easter baskets and prayers from Sandy.*

   o *Homebound elderly ladies received shopping services and fellowship from Catherine.*

   o *Melvin's sons grew closer to him and were introduced to the Bible.*

- Everyone benefited from Pat giving up hurtful wisecracks. Disaster victims and the audience benefited from Pat's comedy performance.

- At-risk babies and untold others benefited from Lee's advocacy for pro-life and health care legislation. A troubled teen will be encouraged by Lee's mentoring.

- The Sacrifice Support Group and Lee's confirmation student benefited from Sandy's prayers.

- Gina's giving up fear brought subtle benefits to the entire Sacrifice Support Group. Pushing herself to speak up, Gina encouraged and gently prodded the others along good paths. She provided material support, too, delivering Sandy's Easter baskets and giving Melvin's family a study Bible.

3. What did each character personally gain from the experience? How did each one grow?

- As Sandy shifted her focus to others, she found relief from job stress and unhealthy snacking. She learned that her prayers are a valuable gift.

- Catherine became less self-indulgent, too. She has no family, so the friendships she developed in her shopping ministry probably filled a lonely void.

- Melvin is closer to his sons. He gained personal insights from his new Bible study and took a big step toward shaking his television habit. He learned that he can be entertained in a more wholesome manner than his adult cable shows.

- Pat gained compassion and self-awareness. She learned kinder ways to express her God-given sense of humor, finding a comedy ministry. She learned to call on the Holy Spirit for help.

- Although Gina appeared to have the least to learn because she was already making a mature Lenten sacrifice, she bloomed into a respected, quietly assertive leader within the group.

- After initially trying to bargain her way out of her impulsive sacrifice commitment, Lee left her "white-collar comfort zone" to mentor a difficult confirmation student. Lee stands to gain a close relationship with both the student and the Holy Spirit. Lee learned that her compassionate heart can be more valuable to the Lord than her professional credentials.

4. Did the six characters feel relieved that their Lenten sacrificial obligation was nearly over?

- ○ *No. They found that their sacrifices were less painful than they expected and that the benefits outweighed their personal discomfort.*

- ○ *They all chose to make the discipline of sacrifice a permanent part of their lives.*

- ○ *They decided to continue meeting for mutual support and encouragement.*

To spread the study program over more shorter sessions, divide Session Five into two sessions, ending the first half here.

If the group is large, Leader may choose to have participants discuss the following questions in breakout groups.

LEADER:

1. Share a summary or highlights of your personal sacrifice experience over the course of this program. How has your sacrifice benefited you? How has it benefited others?

2. Has your way of thinking about Lenten sacrifices been changed by this experience? How?

3. Will you consider continuing your Lenten sacrifice, or some other form of sacrifice, as a permanent discipline in your life? If so, how?

4. Can you apply some insight you've gained during this Lent program to your year-round everyday life? What?

5. Other questions or thoughts to share?

CLOSING BENEDICTION:

We'll close this final session of our Lenten sacrifice study with the Biblical blessing enjoyed by the fictional Sacrifice Support Group:

"God did not appoint us to suffer wrath but to receive salvation through our Lord Jesus Christ. He died for us so that we may live together with him. Therefore encourage one another and build each other up, just as in fact you are doing. Do not put out the Spirit's fire. May God himself, the God of peace, sanctify you through and through. The grace of our Lord Jesus Christ be with you. Amen."

OPTIONAL HANDOUTS

Giving It Up for Lent

Session Two Handout

1. In the first act of *The Sacrifice Support Group*, you met six fictional Christians challenged by their pastor to re-think their ideas about Lenten sacrifice. What did you learn about these characters and their previous Lenten practices?

- o *Sandy*

- o *Catherine*

- o *Melvin*

- o *Pat*

- o *Gina*

- o *Lee*

2. Do you see any truth in Lee's opinion that Christians make "self-serving sacrifices"?

3. What new or improved sacrifices did each member of the group commit to make?

- o *Sandy*
- o *Catherine*
- o *Melvin*
- o *Pat*
- o *Gina*
- o *Lee*

4. Whose sacrifice do you think will be the hardest for him/her to accomplish? Why?

The easiest? Why?

5. Which of these characters' planned sacrifices would pose the most difficulty for you to do? Why?

Which of their sacrifices would pose the least difficulty for you to do? Why?

6. Consider the things that the group is going to give up. How had those things come between them and God?

Between them and other people?

7. The group observed that giving up fear, prejudice, anxiety, indifference, and pride could free individuals to do good things. Can you think of other negative attitudes that hold Christians back from serving God and their neighbors?

8. Can you suggest some good sacrifice choices that were not mentioned in the drama?

9. The fictional Sacrifice Support Group members promised to call one another to account when they slipped up. How would you feel about giving and receiving that kind of input?

Giving It Up for Lent   **Session Three Handout**

1. What are some examples of Lenten sacrifices you've made in the past?

2. Have you felt inspired to make a new or improved Lenten sacrifice commitment this year?

3. What have you chosen to sacrifice? What will you do with the time, treasure, or other resources you release by giving it up? Or does your sacrifice involve doing more rather than giving something up?

4. How do you expect your sacrifice to benefit others?

5. Other questions or thoughts to share?

6. Before our next session, find a passage in the New Testament which provides guidance regarding sacrifice. Bring it in to share with the group.

Giving It Up for Lent   Session Four Handout

1. What form has your Lenten sacrifice taken?

2. Was the cherished thing you gave up coming between you and God? Will giving it up strengthen you and/or your family, church, or community?

3. How does your sacrifice glorify God? Can sacrifices made in secret give glory to God?

4. Have any problems hindered your sacrificial plans? Were they overcome?

5. Has confiding your sacrifice plan to this group or to a trusted friend helped you carry it out?

6. Have you seen God working in your life or the lives of others as a result of your sacrificial acts?

7. What are you learning about yourself during this process? About other people? About God?

8. According to the gospel of John, the last words of Jesus on the cross were a loud cry of victory: "It is finished!" Have you ever felt a sense of spiritual victory upon completing a difficult task in obedience to God's direction?

9. Other questions or thoughts to share?

1. How well did the Sacrifice Support Group characters succeed in carrying out their Lenten sacrifice commitments?

- o *Sandy*

- o *Catherine*

- o *Melvin*

- o *Pat*

- o *Gina*

- o *Lee*

2. How did their Lenten activities benefit others?

- o *Sandy*

- o *Catherine*

- o *Melvin*

- o *Pat*

- o *Gina*

- o *Lee*

3. What did each character personally gain from the experience? How did each one grow?

- o *Sandy*

- o *Catherine*

- o *Melvin*

- o *Pat*

- o *Gina*

- o *Lee*

4. Did the six characters feel relieved that their Lenten sacrificial obligation was nearly over?

Giving It Up for Lent   **Session Five Handout #2**

1. Share a summary or highlights of your personal sacrifice experience over the course of this program. How has your sacrifice benefited you? How has it benefited others?

2. Has your way of thinking about Lenten sacrifices been changed by this experience? How?

3. Will you consider continuing your Lenten sacrifice, or some other form of sacrifice, as a permanent discipline in your life? If so, how?

4. Can you apply some insight you've gained during this Lent program to your year-round everyday life? What?

5. Other questions or thoughts to share?

ACKNOWLEDGMENTS

The weekly Lenten soup and study series that inspired *Giving It Up for Lent* was hosted by four rural New York congregations: Nineveh Presbyterian Church, Harpursville United Methodist Church, Sanitaria Springs United Methodist Church, and North Fenton United Methodist Church. My thanks to everyone who participated, especially the good sports who played our Sacrifice Support Group.

Special thanks to NPC's worship committee for proposing the topic of Lenten sacrifice and to pastors Emrys Tyler (NPC) and Cindy Wenziger (NFUMC) for their contributions to developing the programs for that series.

ABOUT THE AUTHOR

Linda Bonney Olin is a veteran leader of Bible studies and Sunday school programs for adults. She was certified as a lay speaker in the United Methodist Church in 1997. Her writing ministry has produced a wealth of dramas, songs, sermons, puppet plays, and special programs for interdenominational church groups. Her poems, devotions, short fiction, hymns, and Bible study materials have been published in literary and devotional magazines, anthologies, hymnals, and online publications.

Visit www.LindaBonneyOlin.com to contact Linda, learn more about her and her work, and find a variety of resources for ministry, music, and writing. Check the Audio page to listen to examples of the music from her books and her other songs and hymns. Performances of selected songs may be heard on her YouTube channel.

ALSO BY LINDA BONNEY OLIN

Giving It Up for Lent—Workbook: Bible Study, Drama, Discussion

Individual book for study participants. Includes the script of the two-act dramatic comedy *The Sacrifice Support Group,* plus workbook pages corresponding to the Bible passages and discussion questions contained in the leader guide.

The Sacrifice Support Group: A Dramatic Comedy for Lent

Play script only. Two twenty-minute acts.

Now Sings My Soul: New Songs for the Lord

More than a hundred hymns and faith songs with lyrics by Linda Bonney Olin, presented in stanza format for easy reading and also in musical settings. Some feature original music; most are set to classic hymn tunes. Includes indexes of relevant scripture passages and suggested themes/occasions for use in worship.

Songs for the Lord: A Book of Twenty-Four Original Hymns and Faith Songs

A mix of congregational hymns, soulful solos, hand-clapping gospel, and humorous songs. Lyrics and melodies; no piano accompaniment. (Updated versions of some songs from this collection appear with full accompaniment in *Now Sings My Soul*.)

Were You There When They Crucified Our Lord? Meditations on Calvary

A devotional study focusing on individuals and groups who were there the day Jesus Christ was arrested and executed:

- The Roman authorities and the religious leaders
- The twelve
- The women
- The crucified thieves
- and more

Six chapters of scripture readings, meditations, songs, discussion questions, and prayers. Suitable for church programs, small group study, or private reading.

Transformed: 5 Resurrection Dramas

Five one-act plays to read or perform with a small cast. Each play explores how a person close to Jesus was transformed by his resurrection:

- Simon Peter (dramatic comedy)
- John the Apostle (dramatic monologue)
- James the Brother of Jesus (dramatic comedy with five short ensemble songs; plus an alternate interview version)
- Mary the Mother of Jesus (light drama)
- Mary Magdalene (dramatic monologue with optional solo songs)

Each Resurrection Drama also is available as a single-script e-book.

www.ingramcontent.com/pod-product-compliance
Lightning Source LLC
Chambersburg PA
CBHW081545040426
42448CB00015B/3232